Daniel & Lo

Great to know you!

Let's change the world!

Bob Sharpe

2 Cor 5:15

How Your Church Can Change the World

Evangelism by Multiplication

Now may He who supplies seed to the sower, and bread for food, supply and multiply the seed you have sown and increase the fruits of your righteousness,

2 Corinthians 9:10

Bob Sharpe
www.ChangeTheWorldTeam.com

www.ChangeTheWorldTeam.com

ISBN-13: 978-1478207542
ISBN-10: 147820754X

Dedication

Dedicated to the people who influenced my life for God

Rev. Ralph Barteld

He cared enough about me to
lead me to Christ when I was a teenager.
The night I received Christ
he told me to become a soul winner.

Dr. C. Sumner Wemp

His passionate love for the Lord
and his compassionate love for the lost
was truly contagious.

Dr. Jerry Falwell

His example and his preaching led me to see that one church
can make a big difference for Christ in its city
using Saturation Evangelism.

Dr. Elmer Towns

As a young preacher I read his books on growing churches over and over. He was kind enough to meet with me and give me counsel when I was preparing to plant a church in Canada.

Acknowledgements

Special Thanks to:

Jack Parry
Whose help with proofreading
and suggestions for the book were invaluable.

Pastor William Eng
Orange County Chinese Baptist Church, Anaheim, CA
Who unselfishly shared valuable materials and information
concerning the process of evangelism and the Engel Scale.

Pastor Daniel Fan
Mandarin Baptist Church of Temple City, Arcadia, CA
His faithful encouragement and prayers
were just what I needed when I was starting this project.

Pastor Dale Garland
Hemet Valley Baptist Church, Hemet, CA
His wholehearted support and encouragement
spurred me on every step of the way.

Doyle Braden
Retired SBC Director of Missions, Orange County, CA
His constant words of encouragement and
his prayer support mean much to me in this work.

Contents

Introduction: How to Tell the Future

It's not difficult to tell the future. All you have to do is watch where we're going. If we keep on going there, well, we'll get there.

The question is, do we want to go there? Where is your church heading? Do you want it to get there? What will happen when it arrives?

Many churches in North America are slowly dying; many are closing their doors every week. Many other churches are one generation away from extinction, and they're not taking a serious look at the future. It is easy to live in denial.

There is another way we can tell the future. We can tell the future by creating the future ourselves. When we partner with God and diligently plant and water the seed of the Word of God, He will give the increase (1 Corinthians 3:6). Of course it is only God who can give the increase, but He will only give it when we do the planting and watering. We are laborers together with God (1 Cor. 3:9).

We propose an overall Biblical strategy, known as Evangelism by Multiplication that will multiply the effectiveness of our evangelistic efforts. The Five and One Plan, outlined in this book, will give your members the simple baby steps they need to get involved.

This is not a book about church growth. Rather, it is about Kingdom growth in and through your church. Our primary goal is to obey the Great Commission and reach our cities and communities for Christ. It is not a book about how to get a lot of decisions for Christ. It is about reaching the lost, bringing them to salvation in Christ and then about training them become disciples who make disciples who make disciples. When we do it properly, our churches cannot help but grow. If we focus on church growth, we are putting the cart before the horse. If we focus on making disciples who make disciples and building the Kingdom, we are doing God's work in God's way.

It is my prayer that you will catch the vision and create the future God wants for your church and for the people within its reach.

www.ChangeTheWorldTeam.com

Bob Sharpe
Homeland, California, USA
April, 2015

Section 1

What it Looks Like

1: We've Got What they Want!

When I was a student at Moody Bible Institute, a speaker came and told of a young man in Chicago who was working on a graduate degree. One of his research projects was to discover what people really want in life. He spent days on the streets of Chicago with a one-question survey. He asked, ***"Assuming you have your health, what do you want more than anything in life?"***

After getting thousands of answers, he found that the top three things people wanted in life, in this order, were:

1. Love
2. Happiness, or Joy[1]
3. Peace

Where have you heard those words before, in that order?

> But the fruit of the Spirit is love, joy, peace, longsuffering, kindness, goodness, faithfulness, gentleness, self-control. Against such there is no law.
> (Galatians 5:22-23)

---

[1] Christian joy is more than happiness, It is happiness on steroids, so it fits the answer the respondents gave in the survey.

Did you get that? *WE HAVE WHAT THEY WANT!* We have it in Christ! It's when we are experiencing the Fruit of the Spirit in our lives. It is important for us, as believers, to stay close to the Lord in our relationship with Him so we can enjoy all the benefits of the Christian life.

Do they know we have what they want? They will if we are in love with Jesus and we are living victorious Christian lives. They will see it in us if they are around us and we have meaningful relationships with them.

That's how I came to Christ. I had been raised in a liberal Protestant church that did not believe the Bible was the Word of God, and that did not believe the Gospel. (There are many Protestant churches like that today). All they taught was rules, rites, rituals and religion. Then, at age 16, I met some teenagers who were enjoying abundant lives in Christ. It surprised me. Their lives impressed me so much that after three days I became one of them. I received Christ, and He changed my life totally.

Before that, I had a misconception of what Christianity and the Christian life is. Most people do. They don't realize it is a real relationship with the great God Who created the universe. In North America and Europe many people look upon church as boring rituals and useless rules. They don't see any reason why church should be a part of their lives.

We have what people want in life! They just don't know it, and too often we don't show it.

> Oh, taste and see that the LORD is good; Blessed is the man who trusts in Him!
> (Psalm 34:8)

The goodness of God satisfies and fills us when we walk with Him. The goodness of God also leads people to repentance and eternal life.

> . . . the goodness of God leads you to repentance (Romans 2:4)

When people see the goodness of God exhibited in our lives, they notice. That's what can make them receptive to the Gospel when we share with them.

Many people might hate what we stand for. They might hate the Gospel. They may have given up on church. They might listen to the news media when it says that Christians are haters. But they need to know we have what they want. In many people, it will arouse their curiosity, and many will be open to listening to us share the Gospel. Many will become believers in time.

When we are living victorious Christian lives, when we are living with integrity, when we are filled with the peace and joy of the Lord, and when we sincerely love people, they will notice. Not only has God called us to live on a higher plane, He gives us the power to do so with joy and peace of mind. When they see the Fruit of the Spirit in our lives, some will be curious, some will want what we have, and many will be more willing to listen to us when we share the Gospel with them.

That is what the Lord meant when He said,

> "You are the light of the world. . . . Let your light so shine before men, that they may see your good works and glorify your Father in heaven.
> (Matthew 5:14-16)

95% of all the people who come to Christ do so because of the influence of a Christian in their lives. When we are really experiencing the abundant life in Christ, He can make a big impact on the people we know through our lives.

It has been said that you are the only Bible some people will ever read. Our lives should give an accurate picture of Who Jesus is, and what He can do in our lives.

A few years ago I wrote a book on network marketing. The book became a best-seller on Amazon. All through the book I added drawings to illustrate what I was writing about. As people bought the book and read it, I was surprised at the comments I got. While most people thought the content of my writing was good, I got a lot more comments on the pictures than on the writing! The pictures got people's attention far more than my "words of wisdom." (I plan to add drawings to future editions of this book).

When we represent Jesus to the world, our lives are the pictures, and the words we use to share the Gospel with them are the words of the book. If the pictures in our lives are good, they will attract people to the message. The pictures our lives present must match the words we share. When we talk about Jesus, our lives must illustrate Jesus. Our lives don't tell the story, but our lives will make the story interesting, believable and compelling.

All around us people are living broken lives. Marriages are in turmoil. Their children are in trouble. Suicides are up. People are doing desperate things. Many of our neighbors have no hope. Many others are living humdrum lives with no sense of purpose.

When you go to the bank, that smiling bank teller may be distressed about a broken relationship. Your insurance agent may be distressing over a wayward daughter. Your friendly hairstylist may be worried over financial problems since her husband is out of work. There is hope in Christ. We have the answer. Some of them might open up on the spot if you show them a little love, a kind word and an invitation to church.

Pastor Gil De La Rosa, of New Hope Community Church in El Monte, California told me about a lady who was passing his church one day. When she saw the sign "New Hope Community Church," she stopped and walked into the church office.

When Pastor Gil talked with her, she told him, "I've lost all hope in life. I saw your sign that said 'New Hope.' Can you give me hope?"

Gil pointed her to the God of all Hope. She was not alone. There are multitudes of people like her. They don't know where or how to find answers to the challenges of life.

Most people won't tell you they are looking for something in life. But, deep down in their hearts, many of them are. They're out there - everywhere. Let's recommit ourselves to give them the Answer.

Recently, when I was getting my hair cut, I asked my barber if she went to church anywhere.

"Oh, I'm Catholic, but I don't go any more," she replied.

I invited her to church, and I was surprised at her response. She was really appreciative. She thanked me over and over for inviting her.

A few years ago I was having lunch with Pastor Glenn Layne, in a restaurant in Temple City, California. When the server came with our food, Glenn told her, "We are Christians, and we will be praying over our food. Is there anything in your life that you would like us to pray about for you?"

Her eyes got big and she held back her tears as she opened up to us about some major challenges she was facing. She was very appreciative that we showed her that we cared for her. Glenn left a Gospel tract with a big tip. He got her name and said he would go back and follow up with her later.

We are here to care for people, to love them with the love that God gives us, and ultimately to lead them to Christ. It's not about us. It's about them, and God's love for them.

The world calls it *proselytization;* God calls it *evangelism.* There is a difference. *Proselytization* is the act of trying to get outsiders to join your church. *Evangelism,* on the other hand, is sharing the Good News of Jesus so that people can become part of the family of God. Of course you want the new believers to join your church if they live in your area. But it is infinitely more important that they become members of God's family, even if they get involved in another good church.

Evangelism is not what you do TO people;
Evangelism is what you do FOR people.

2: The Process of Evangelism

God's desire is for us to be fruitful. He will grow the fruit in us when we are living close to Christ. The fruit of the Spirit is how God develops our lives. As we walk in the Spirit, God grows the fruit of the Spirit in us.

> I say then: Walk in the Spirit, and you shall not fulfill the lust of the flesh. (Galatians 5:16)

The fruit of the Spirit is all of God. It is our Christian character and our ability to enjoy God and to enjoy life in harmony with His purpose in us. The fruit of the Spirit in us attracts the interest and/or curiosity of some of the unbelievers we engage with.

The fruit of our service shows in the new believers we bring into the Kingdom. That fruit comes from God, too, but He does not give it until we do our part. That's how God works. He gives the harvest to the farmer, but the farmer must plant and tend to the field, or there is no harvest.

> I planted, Apollos watered, but God gave the increase. (1 Corinthians 3:6)

Evangelism is more than a "one-shot deal." There are actually three stages in the process. Two of the stages are listed in 2 Corinthians 3:6 - planting and watering. The other stage is reaping the harvest, or bringing a person "across the line" to faith in Christ. When we are involved in evangelism, we will be involved in all three stages at times.

Planting the Seed

The seed of the Word of God is planted during a person's first exposure to the Gospel. Many North Americans have been exposed to church and religion, but large numbers of them have never been exposed to the Gospel. Not everyone is ready to respond to the love of God the first time he or she hears the Gospel. God can use the exposure to bring them closer to the point where they will ultimately receive Christ, however.

Watering the Seed

This takes place when people have subsequent exposures to Christians and the Gospel. These are the influences that can cause them to think about the claims of Christ and move them closer to the point where they will become Christians. There are many things that can water the seed and bring them closer to Christ. Some of these things could be:

- Visiting a church service
- Watching a Gospel TV program
- An act of kindness by a Christian
- Hearing a Christian testimony
- Getting their questions answered
- A Bible study

- Being around Christians who are experiencing the joy of the Lord
- Attending a funeral

Charting their Progress with the Engel Scale

The **Engel Scale** was developed by James F. Engel as a way to represent the journey a person takes from no knowledge of God through to spiritual maturity as a Christian. The model is used to illustrate the various decision-making steps that a person may go through in the process of becoming a Christian. When we help a person move closer to becoming a Christian, we are watering the seed.

It involves loving and respecting them, sharing, listening, helping people find answers to their questions and guiding them into faith in Christ. For many people it takes time and multiple exposures to the Gospel.

Remember, we are not looking for quick decisions, but for people who will truly repent and become life-long followers of Christ. Sometimes God will bring people our way who will be ready to receive Christ immediately.

God's Timing vs. Their Timing

Yes, it is urgent that they get saved as soon as possible. We know that, but they don't. Even though God's time is now (2 Corinthians 6:2), they may not see the need, and they won't repent until they are ready (Acts 26:28). If we cannot bring them to salvation when we talk with them, maybe we can bring them from one or two steps closer to repentance. When we do that, we are "watering the seed." (1 Corinthians 3:6). God might bring someone else along to move them closer or lead them to Christ, or He might give us the opportunity at another time.

Engel Scale

God's Role	Our Role		Man's Response
General Revelation	Proclamation	-8	Awareness of Supreme Being, but no effective knowledge of Gospel
Conviction		-7	Initial Awareness of Gospel
		-6	Awareness of Gospel Fundamentals
		-5	Grasp of Implications of Gospel
		-4	Positive Attitude Toward Gospel
		-3	Personal Problem Recognition
		-2	Decision to Act
	Persuasion	-1	Repentance and Faith in Christ
REGENERATION			NEW CREATURE IN CHRIST
Sanctification	Follow Up	+1	Post-Decision Evaluation
	Cultivation	+2	Incorporation into Body
		+3	Conceptual and Behavioral Growth
		+4	Communion with God
		+5	Stewardship and Reproduction

Sometimes people are willing to pray the sinner's prayer before they are ready to repent. If we talk them into "praying the prayer" before they understand and believe the Gospel, they will not be saved. It is important to be thorough when we are sharing the Gospel. If they are not ready to receive Christ, God can still use us to bring them one step closer to salvation. If we push them into "praying the prayer" before they are ready, we will think they really got saved when nothing happened. They will be disappointed with their experience because nothing will have happened in their lives, and they will be harder to reach in the future.

This does not mean we should not diligently try to lead a person to Christ when we are talking to them. It means that we should not push them when they are obviously not ready.

If all we do is bring a person one step closer to knowing Christ, we have not failed in evangelism. We have done our job of watering the seed.

God Gives the Increase

When a person is born again, it is God's doing. We share the Gospel. We love people, encourage them and answer their questions along their spiritual journey. All during the process, God is drawing them to Jesus (John 6:44), and the Holy Spirit is convicting them of their sin (John 16:8-11). We are laborers together with God in the process. We are working with God the Father and the Holy Spirit to bring people to Jesus. We must do what we can do. Only God can do what He does in preparing a person's heart for salvation. We can convince people to make a decision or pray a prayer.

It takes more than that. Only God can draw them and produce the New Birth.

He will give us the fruit when we become the people He wants to make of us, and when we do the work He has called every believer to do. Any believer can be a fruitful servant of the Lord. It is true that some will be more fruitful in evangelism than others. He gives different people different gifts and abilities. It is not important for you to be what another believer can be in Christ. It is important for you to be everything God wants to make of you.

Even so, every believer has the responsibility to bring others to Christ. Later in this book we will explain the Five and One Plan, which will make it easy for any believer to get started and become fruitful.

3: Evangelism by the Numbers

> Then the word of God spread, and the number of the disciples multiplied greatly in Jerusalem, and a great many of the priests were obedient to the faith.
> (Acts 6:7)

> Then the churches throughout all Judea, Galilee, and Samaria had peace and were edified. And walking in the fear of the Lord and in the comfort of the Holy Spirit, they were multiplied.
> (Acts 9:31)
>
> But the word of God grew and multiplied.
> (Acts 12:24)

Why did the church grow so quickly in New Testament times? It is because the number of disciples was multiplying. There are a number of factors that made the church multiply, and we'll examine them later in the book. First, let's look at the math and see why it was so powerful.

Most churches today grow by addition. They add a new member or two every now and then, and they hope they will add more members than they lose. This Addition Model of church growth is so common that pastors will often talk about the number of "additions" they had in a given month or year. Most churches and pastors are satisfied with the

Addition Model. If the early church would have used this model of growth and evangelism, it would have died out in the First Century.

Instead we read in the Book of Acts that the number of disciples *multiplied*. Multiplication does not exclude additions, it creates multiple additions.

> Then those who gladly received his word were baptized; and that day about three thousand souls were added to them.
> (Act 2:41)

> . . . And the Lord added to the church daily those who were being saved.
> (Act 2:47)

The Difference Between Multiplication and Addition

Addition, by itself, yields slow growth. Many churches experience such slow growth (or no growth) that it is a big event when someone joins the church. All too often the number of people joining barely keeps up with the number of people leaving. Sometimes it doesn't even do that.

How Addition Works
10 + 10 + 10 + 10 + 10 = **50**

When a church operates with the Biblical multiplication strategy, however, exciting things begin to happen. It is an exciting event when a member brings his or her first person to eternal life in Jesus. Whenever this happens, you can celebrate with them publicy in the morning service. Leading their first soul to Christ is a very important milestone in anyone's Christian life. Your people will be revitalized when they see how God is using them to affect the eternal destiny of the people they know. It will usually start with a few people in the church, and then it can spread throughout the entire congregation.

In 1871, it is told that a cow kicked over a kerosene lamp and started a fire in a barn in Chicago. The fire spread out until almost the entire city burned to the ground. The Holy Spirit fires of revival and evangelism can spread rapidly and change a city for Christ. Start the fire burning and help it spread throughout your church.

How Multiplication Works

10 x 10 x 10 x 10 x 10 = **100,000**

The Biblical Basis for Multiplication

God used people to populate the earth by multiplication (Genesis 1:28). The words *multiply* and *multiplied* appear 91 times in the Bible. 57 of those times they refer to the multiplication of people - to populate the earth, to expand the nation of Israel and to grow the church. God uses multiplication. Do we practice multiplication God's way?

When we plan to multiply, we are planning to do God's work in God's way.

> And the things that you have heard from me among many witnesses, commit these to faithful men who will be able to teach others also.
> (2 Timothy 2:2)

Paul's admonition to his protégé, Timothy, was to take the things that he had taught him and to teach those things to faithful men. The job of these faithful men was to take those things and teach them to others. This is how multiplication works in the church.

How Multiplication Causes Growth

Starting with 100 Committed Christians

Year	Number
Year 1	100
Year 2	200
Year 3	400
Year 4	800
Year 5	1,600
Year 6	3,200
Year 7	6,400
Year 8	12,800
Year 9	25,600
Year 10	51,200

Think of what would happen if 100 members of your church would each win one person to Christ this year, and they would get them into the church and disciple them to maturity in Christ. Then the original 100 plus the 100 new believers would do the same thing the following year. And the following year, etc.

Could that happen? Why not? God multiplied the church in the past. He can do it again.

How can we see God do it again?

1. We need to believe God for big things.

He is a big God. He created the big universe. He delights to do big things. He challenged us to believe Him for big things. Do you believe Him?

> 'Call to Me, and I will answer you, and show you great and mighty things, which you do not know.'
> (Jeremiah 33:3)

2. We need to realize it is God's will for multitudes of people to come to Christ.

> who desires all men to be saved and to come to the knowledge of the truth.
> (1Timothy 2:4)

3. We need to commit ourselves and our churches to make the Great Commission our priority for the rest of our lives. (Matthew 28:19-20; Acts 1:8)

4. We need to equip our people in our churches to do the work of ministering to the non-Christians within their spheres of influence.

> And He Himself gave some *to be* apostles, some prophets, some evangelists, and some pastors and teachers, for the equipping of the saints for the work of ministry, for the edifying of the body of Christ,
> (Ephesians 4:11-12)

5. We need to plan and implement the strategy that will latch on to God's plan of multiplication. We need to do it on purpose and never stop doing it until God calls us home.

4: Multiplication through Addition

People come to faith in Christ individually, one person at a time. When the 3,000 people were converted on the Day of Pentecost, it was not a mass conversion. It was 3,000 individual conversions.

The real multiplication takes place when we multiply the number of Christians who take the command to reproduce seriously.

There is a Scriptural principle that it is God's will for each Christian to bring one or two people per year to faith in Christ. To many people, it seems like a huge mountain to climb, but in reality it is not that big of a task for believers who are properly equipped, motivated and supported every week by the church. This cannot merely be a church program. It must be the priority that permeates every aspect of the church's life. *If we are not actively equipping and encouraging our people in this task, what are we doing in church?*

In the Parable of the Sower, the Lord explained that the sower would encounter four kinds of ground as he plants the seed of the Word of God. The first three types of ground represent the hearers with different reactions to the Gospel when they hear it. Some don't understand and reject the Gospel. Others show varying degrees of genuine interest but are never genuinely born again.

> "Therefore hear the parable of the sower: When anyone hears the word of the kingdom, and does not understand *it,* then the wicked *one* comes and snatches away what was sown in his heart. This is he who received seed by the wayside. But he who received the seed on stony places, this is he who hears the word and immediately receives it with joy; yet he has no root in himself, but endures only for a while. For when tribulation or persecution arises because of the word, immediately he stumbles. Now he who received seed among the thorns is he who hears the word, and the cares of this world and the deceitfulness of riches choke the word, and he becomes unfruitful. But he who received seed on the good ground is he who hears the word and understands *it,* who indeed bears fruit and produces: some a hundredfold, some sixty, some thirty."
> (Matthew 13:18-23)

The people who are represented by the "good ground," however, are the people who are genuinely born again.

When a farmer plants a field, he expects each seed to grow into a plant that will yield many seeds. That is how the farmer makes his living, and that is how we have food to eat. It is because the seed multiplies itself. Seeds naturally grow and multiply when they are properly planted, watered and fertilized. It is the law of nature.

In the parable, Jesus is saying that the good ground represents the person who comes to know Him. He says the seed in the good ground is expected produce a multiple of 30, 60 or 100-fold.

Jesus is telling us that the people represented by the good ground are the people who get saved through the preaching or witnessing of the sower. God is expecting them to reproduce 30, 60 or 100-fold. That means God's expectation is that a normal Christian should bring 30, 60 or 100 people to Christ in his or her lifetime. (Of course, if a person comes to Christ late in life, that number would be lower). If we take 30 to 100 as God's norm, that would calculate to one or two people per year.

If you became a Christian when you were young, and if you live to a normal age of 70 to 80 years, God expects you to bring approximately 30 to 100 people into the Kingdom during your lifetime. Are you on target for that goal?

Our job as pastors and leaders, then, is to be fruitful in evangelism ourselves, and to lead our flocks by our example, as well as by our training. We need to pray daily for our members to each bear the fruit of evangelism every year. Then we need to equip, motivate and remind them every week.

Since we know that it is God's will for us, we can pray in confidence that He will hear us and that He will answer our prayer to give us fruit for our labor for Him.

> Now this is the confidence that we have in Him, that if we ask anything according to His will, He hears us. And if we know that He hears us, whatever we ask, we know that we have the petitions that we have asked of Him.
> (1 John 5:14-15)

We also know it is His will for people to come to Christ.

> who desires all men to be saved and to come to the knowledge of the truth.
> (1Timothy 2:4)

We can pray in confidence for His will to be accomplished.

> Your kingdom come. Your will be done on earth as *it is* in heaven.
> (Matthew 6:10)

Please stop reading right now for a moment, claim God's promises and ask Him to help you win one or more souls to Christ this year. Pray every day for His fruit in your life.

If you are a pastor or a leader in your church, set the example in evangelism. Pray that it will catch on. Then fan the flame, so that that many others in your church will follow.

God is in the fruit-growing business (John 15). You are the fruit He grew as the result of somebody's seed-sowing ministry when you became a Christian. He wants to grow the fruit of the Spirit in you, and the fruit of service through you. As His life flows to the branch (you) from the Vine (Jesus), it can't help but bear much fruit and glorify God.

When multiple people in our churches are consistently witnessing and bearing fruit, we will begin to see multiplication as increasing numbers of people are brought into the Kingdom of God regularly.

We need to equip our members with an easy way to take the baby steps to get started so they can see that God can use them in evangelism. If we don't give them the baby steps, many of them will never start, and they will live unfruitful lives.

This is why we created the free Evangelism by Multiplication app. You can download it for Android or Apple phones and tablets free in the Google Play Store or the Apple App Store. The name is *Evangelism by Multiplication,* and the logo is a butterfly.

If you know how to use QR codes, you can use one of these to download and install the app to your device:

Android

Apple

More on the app in another chapter.

5: An Effective Model of Multiplication

For more than 80 years, The Navigators organization has been a very effective ministry of winning people to Christ and discipling them to spiritual maturity. Dawson Trotman, their founder, understood the principle of multiplication and practiced it.

Dawson died in 1956 while trying to rescue a drowning swimmer in a camp in New York State. He died the same way he lived - by giving of himself for others. Billy Graham preached the funeral. In his funeral message, he said, "I think Dawson Trotman has personally touched more lives [for Christ's sake] than anybody that I have ever known."

Why did he touch so many lives? It was because he practiced multiplication on purpose. He reached others for Christ. Then he trained them to become active Christ-followers and reach others for Christ, so they could train them. He built The Navigators on that model. When we reach others for Christ and then disciple them so that they can reach and disciple others, we are multiplying our influence for the Lord.

As of 2015, the Navigators has more than 4,600 staff members of 70 nationalities in more than 100 countries, over 170 languages, and among 220 peoples. It all happened because of the Biblical multiplication principle practiced and taught by Dawson Trotman years ago.

Dawson Trotman and Multiplication

(Taken from www.thenavigators.org)

Dawson began teaching high school students and local Sunday school classes these principles. In 1933, he and his friends extended their work to sailors in the U.S. Navy. There, Dawson taught sailor Les Spencer the foundations of Christian growth. They spent many hours together praying, studying the Bible, and memorizing Scripture. When one of Spencer's shipmates asked him the secret of his changed life,[2] Spencer brought the man to Trotman: "Teach him what you taught me," he said.

"You teach him!" Trotman responded. And the 2 Timothy 2:2 vision was strengthened.

Spencer did teach the sailor, and soon the two men were meeting with others. Eventually, 125 men on their ship, the U.S.S. West Virginia, were growing in Christ and actively sharing their faith. **By the end of World War II, thousands of men on ships and bases around the world were learning the principles of spiritual multiplication by the person-to-person teaching of God's word.** (Emphasis mine).

How Multiplication Works in the Local Church

If a small church has one pastor, and if the pastor is the only person in the church who witnesses for the Lord, not much evangelism will take place. On the rare occasions that a

---

[2] This is how the Fruit of the Spirit can attract the attention of unbelievers. (Comment mine).

new person comes to the Lord, he or she will look around the church and see that no one else is witnessing. The new believer will learn a bad lesson by example.

Let's say the pastor equips 10 people in that small church to effectively witness for the Lord. That church becomes potentially 10 times more potent to reach the community for Christ. The number of people sharing the Gospel has multiplied 10 fold.

The primary task of the professional ministry in the church is to equip the members to do the work of the ministry.

> And He Himself gave some *to be* apostles, some prophets, some evangelists, and some pastors and teachers, for the equipping of the saints for the work of ministry, for the edifying of the body of Christ, (Ephesians 4:11-12)

Pastor, how well have you and your ministry staff equipped your people? if you are not equipping your people to effectively share the Gospel with unbelievers, you are not doing your job! No problem. You can repent and start today! While it is important to teach the Bible, it is also important to DO the Bible.

The next section of this book will give you the track to run on so you can bring your church to the next level in usefulness for the Master. Remember, this is God's will for your church, so He will be there to help you every step of the way.

J. Paul Getty built an empire in the oil business and became the richest man in the world in his day. He had thousands of employees working for his enterprise. He was known for saying, "I'd rather have 1% of the effort of 100 men than 100% of my own effort." I would rather train 100 of my members to each win one soul to Christ this year than to win 100 myself. Would you?

The strategy of evangelism by multiplication happens when multiple members of our churches bring people to Christ regularly, and these new believers are discipled. Adopt the simple plan, described later in this book, yourself and teach it to your members. We call it the Five and One Plan.

We have seen the Scriptural precedence, the command of the Lord and the practical strategy of equipping our members to be fruitful witnesses for Christ. Why is it, then, that this is not the priority in the majority of churches?

Growing Churches and Stagnant Churches

During the 1970's, Dr. Elmer Towns, of Liberty University, wrote a series of books on the effective churches of the US at the time. I read and reread all of these books as I worked to build a church with a vision to reach the whole city for Christ.

One of the things that hit me over and over as I read these books is that these churches were serious about evangelism. They trained their people to share the Gospel. They encouraged their people weekly. They had multiple outreach programs. They expected their staff members to be soul winners. They included an evangelistic appeal in every service. They were led by pastors with a big vision to reach their cities for Christ.

The culture has changed much since the 1970's, and to be effective in reaching people for Christ, we have had to adapt to the changing culture. While some of the methods we used then are no longer effective, the basic principle of Evangelism by Multiplication transcends any culture. It worked spectacularly well in the First Century. It worked in the 1970's. It works today.

The churches that are on the cutting edge of reaching their cities for Christ today are extremely focused on outreach and evangelism. They are doing evangelism and discipleship on purpose.

Evangelism Does Not Happen by Accident.

One of my friends, Doyle Braden, was the Director of Missions for the Orange County (California) Southern Baptist Association in the 1980's when Rick Warren started Saddleback Church. As Director of Missions, Doyle frequently shared a meal with Rick in the early days of the church. Doyle told me that Rick Warren was one of the most focused preachers he had ever known. It was that focus on reaching the lost and building the church that enabled him to build one of the largest and most influential churches in North America. You will see that when you read Rick's book, *The Purpose Driven Church.*[3]

There are many churches that claim that evangelism is important, but they often give more importance to other things. The priority of evangelism tends to slip downward in

[3] Warren, Rick. *The Purpose Driven Church.* Grand Rapids: Zondervan, 1995

importance until it all but disappears. They give lip service to evangelism, but that is all. No wonder churches are dying. And many others will die when the current generation of members dies off.

The churches that are making an impact on their communities are the churches that are totally serious about equipping their members to make an impact. A church with 100 members who are consistently making disciples is a powerful force for Christ in its city.

Five Kinds of Churches

1. Churches that do not evangelize.
2. Churches that talk about evangelism and dabble in it.
3. Churches that get decisions for Christ, but do not grow.
4. Churches that are effective in evangelism
5. Churches that evangelize by Multiplication

What kind of church is your church? What kind of church do you think God wants it to be?

Operating Evangelistically

How much does your church emphasize and do evangelism? That does not mean that the church does nothing but evangelism. It means that everything the church does should have an evangelistic flavor whenever possible.

In his book, *Organic Outreach,*[4] Kevin Harney, Lead Pastor of Shoreline Community Church in Monterey, California, suggests that we look at the things we do for our people and offer them for people in the community. He calls it the "Two Degree Rule."

His previous church had made a practice of bringing meals to people in times of emergency. For example, if a family has a member in the hospital, the people in his church would take turns bringing hot meals to the family. When they adopted the Two Degree Rule, they started doing it for non-Christians in the community. It built bridges to the people they were trying to reach.

What things are you doing well that you could use to build bridges in your community?

Do you have a men's breakfast in your church? Encourage your men to invite their friends. The breakfast does not need to be an evangelistic event, but you can use it to build bridges of friendship with the men who come. Pray that God will use it to move them closer to salvation. You can have a mildly evangelistic appeal at the breakfast. We don't want them to think we are trying to "draw the net" to win them to Christ every time we see them. We want them to know that we are genuine, ordinary people who have found the Answer to life, that we care about them, and we are willing to share it (Him) with them.

Recently Rafael Cruz, father of U.S. Senator Ted Cruz, told me about his conversion. He had been living in Alberta, Canada, and he was in the oil industry. He was a heavy

---

[4] Harney, Kevin. *Organic Outreach.* Grand Rapids: Zondervan, 2009

drinker. He and his wife were separated, and he moved to Houston. Someone invited him to a Bible study. He went, and he noticed the people there had a peace in their hearts that he hadn't seen before. God used that peace and the love they showed him to draw him to Christ. Shortly afterward he received Christ and began to experience the love and peace he saw in the others. A little while later he was reunited with his family.

Do you have a ladies' fellowship program, a youth group, or other groups and activities in your church? Give them an evangelistic purpose. Encourage your people to invite their friends and use the activities to build bridges with the ultimate purpose of bringing them to the Savior.

Always have the goal of moving people one or two steps closer to salvation and bringing them "across the line." It is not enough to bring visitors to the activities. Your purpose is to ultimately lead them to Christ, so you must always be doing things on purpose to lead them closer to their salvation.

How much time in your prayer meetings is devoted to praying for lost people to come to Christ? Do you pray for your church to be more effective in attracting people to the Savior? Do you pray for your people to become soul winners during the services and the prayer meetings of the church? This type of prayer in the public meetings of the church has two effects. First, it brings God into the picture. Second, it leads your people to pray evangelistically. Both are important.

Budget for Evangelism

How much does your church budget for evangelism? Some churches spend more on music than they do on evangelism. Music is important, but it is not the Great Commission. Churches that only give lip service to evangelism don't put their money where their mouths are. Many leaders recommend allocating 10% of your church budget for evangelism and discipleship of the new believers that God gives you. You may need to cut other things out of the budget for a while. However, as God gives fruit to your evangelism ministry, your attendance will grow and your offerings will increase.

The evangelism portion of your church budget can fund such things as:

1. Evangelistic events
2. Evangelism training for members
3. Attendance at evangelism conferences for the pastor and leaders
4. Advertising for evangelistic events
5. Gospel tracts, brochures and booklets
6. Mailers to new residents
7. Gospels of John
8. Bibles
9. Gift bags for church visitors
10. Expense account for the pastor and designated staff members to take church visitors and evangelism prospects to lunch. Lunch meetings can be especially effective for reaching businesspeople.

6: The Five and One Plan

There is a way you can have an important part in changing the world without doing great exploits, spending a lot of money or using a lot of effort. You can do it by changing a small part of your world once every year. You can set up part of a chain reaction that will multiply your effort and make a significant change during your lifetime. It all starts with prayer and a commitment on your part.

The change you would make in your world is to pray for five non-Christians in your sphere of influence to be saved. Make a commitment to God that you will spend a few minutes every day to pray for these five people. This is not mainly a book about evangelistic techniques. It is a book about partnering together with God and engaging with people to introduce them to the God who loves them. God brought these non-Christians into your life for a purpose. They are your responsibility.

Tom Mercer, pastor of High Desert Church in Victorville, CA, has repeatedly stated that 95% of all the people who have ever come to Christ did so on the influence and witness of someone they know[5]. These are the easiest people for you to reach, because they are in a position to see what Christ has been doing in your life, to change it for the

---

[5] Mercer, Tom. *8 to 15 The World Is Smaller than You Think.* Victorville, CA: Oikos Books, 2009, 2017.

better. They are also the easiest people to share Christ with if you know how. High Desert Church has grown to an attendance of 15,000 under his leadership of equipping his people.

The second part of this commitment is to believe God to use you to bring one person to Christ this year. Commit to praying, learning and doing everything you can to lead at least one person to Christ, or to bring them to an evangelistic event where they will come to know Him. Commit to being on the lookout for people you can reach. Ask God to help you win at least one soul to Christ. Believe God for our one person.

Your List of Five People

My Five and One List

1. Betty Jones
2. Richard Chang
3. Sam Smith
4. Hector Gomez
5. Mary Johnson

Heavenly Father, please help me bring at least one person to faith in Christ this year. AMEN

who desires all men to be saved and to come to the knowledge of the truth. (I Timothy 2:4)

Now this is the confidence that we have in Him, that if we ask anything according to His will, He hears us. And if we know that He hears us, whatever we ask, we know that we have the petitions that we have asked of Him. (I John 5:14-15)

www.AndrewEffect.com

Ask God to burden you for the five people you will pray for. If your spouse or children are not Christians, you can put them on the list, but don't count them as part of the five. You will be praying for their salvation anyway.

Do not put elected officials or famous people on this list unless you know them personally, and they know you. It is important to pray for them too - especially your elected officials - but you are only putting people you know and can talk to on this list.

Put the list in your Bible. You might want to make copies of the list on sticky notes and put them in places where you will be reminded to pray for your five. You could put one on the bathroom mirror so you can pray while you are shaving, brushing your teeth or putting on your makeup. You could put another one by your computer monitor and another on the dashboard of your car. Pray for them as you go about your daily activities. Also take a special time just to pray for them during your quiet time.

A number of pastors in Southern California set the alarms on their cell phones to sound at 3:16 PM every day as a reminder to pray for their five people. Why 3:16? It's symbolic for John 3:16. There's nothing magic about the time. If 3:16 is not a good time for you, you can set it for another time every day.

As you pray fervently for your five people, God will work in their hearts. He may bring about circumstances in their lives that make them realize they need help. He may put thoughts in their minds about God and their need to know Him. They might start asking you questions about God. They might begin to open up to you, even though they had been closed in the past. Prayer can do mighty things in the lives of the people we are praying for. I've seen it over and over.

It might take a few weeks or a few years, or even longer, but as you are praying for them, God is working on their hearts. This is not a guarantee that they will be saved, because God, in His sovereignty, gave each of us a free will to decide what we are going to do with Him. He will not force anyone to be saved. He will only speak to their hearts of their need for salvation.

Don't give up if you don't see any response. Remember, God is quick to save, but people are slow to respond. Salvation only takes an instant, but a person could be putting God off for years before his or her day of salvation comes. Their road to salvation can be long and drawn out. I prayed for one of my family members for 41 years before she came to Christ.

While some people will come closer to salvation as you pray, others may actually harden their hearts. We cannot make their decision for them, and God won't make it for them. They must come to the cross on their own volition as God is working in their lives.

Believe God for One Person to Come to Christ

As witnesses for Christ, God wants to use us to bring people to Him for salvation. He wants to give you fruit in personal evangelism. He wants to use you to participate in His grand plan of world evangelism, right there in your corner of the world.

Every week God brings people who need Jesus into your life. They're everywhere. They are your neighbors, your co-workers, your bosses, your friends, your classmates, your teachers and the people you do business with. These are your naturals because you are in contact with them regularly. They know you, they like you and they trust you. Normally the five people on your list will come from this group of "naturals."

When you pray every day for God to use you to win a person to Christ this year, He may save one or more of the people on your list. He may bring someone else into your life that you can lead to Christ. He may do both. Always be on the lookout for someone who will listen. Pray for the wisdom to see when God brings these people across your path.

A few years ago, I put a business friend on my Five and One List and started praying for him. He was an inactive member of a church that did not preach the Gospel. One day we had lunch together. I shared my testimony with him. He listened politely. Several months later I called him to tell him I would be in his area again. I wanted to schedule lunch with him again.

During the conversation he said, "Bob, we started going to church."

I asked, "Really? What church?"

I assumed that he went back to his old church. Then he said, Christ Church of the Valley, which is a good Bible teaching church in his area.

"Wonderful!" I exclaimed. "How did you end up going there?"

"Our neighbor invited us. We went, and we could sense a special power as soon as we went in. All three of us received Christ."

I had been praying for him to be saved. I was trying to schedule a time to witness to him, and his neighbor beat me to the punch. Do you think I mind?

When I was in college, I spent one summer working at McLouth Steel Co. in Trenton, Michigan. One of my co-workers was a committed Christian who spent hours memorizing Scripture by the chapter. At work he was always sharing his faith, and he led a number of co-workers to Christ. One day, as we were talking about evangelism. He told me,

Brother Bob, God will give you souls.
You just have to want 'em bad enough. [sic]

God does that. Do you really want to lead someone to Christ this year? You just have to love Him strongly enough, and you have to want to win a soul badly enough. It is God's will for you to bear fruit for Him. If we pray according to God's will, He will hear and answer our prayer.

Of course, faith without works is dead. God will not do for us what we are supposed to do, but He will help us get it done when we do our part. God won't work through us if we are not working in His harvest field.

Start With Easy Steps

If you have never led anyone to Christ before, start by inviting one of the people on your list to church or to an evangelistic event. It is easy to invite a person to an event. How many times have you invited a friend to a movie or a baseball game? It doesn't take a special skill. All you have to do is open your mouth.

Do not pre-judge people. All too often we prejudge people and talk ourselves out of inviting friends to church. A few years ago I was training some people in our church. As I was talking to one of the ladies, I mentioned the name of her friend. "Oh, she won't come," the lady said. "She's Buddhist."

"You'll never know until you invite her," I answered.

When you invite a person to church, be ready to share your testimony. There are times that a simple invitation to church will arouse curiosity and a willing ear to hear what God has done in your life. If you are just starting out and you're too nervous to share your testimony, invite them anyway. The testimony can come later if necessary.

When you invite a friend to church, offer to pick them up if at all possible.

Here are some interesting statistics:

- About 10% of the people you invite will come to church
- 100% of the people you bring will come

Learn to Do More and Stretch Your Wings

The word *Disciple* means "learner." As followers of Christ we are learners for the rest of our lives. There are certain things you will learn:

1. How to present your testimony
2. How to present the plan of salvation clearly and convincingly
3. How to answer the questions non-Christians commonly ask
4. How to start a conversation with a stranger and turn it to spiritual things
5. How to handle a hard question when you don't know the answer

What to Do After You Lead a Person to Christ

Babies need to be cared for, fed, loved and protected. They need to be placed in an environment where they can grow. When you lead a person to Christ, your babe in Christ needs the same care. Invite them to the class for new believers in your church. Help them make friends in the church so they will have other people to encourage them in their new life in Christ.

Also, immediately help them learn how to share their faith. They have family members and friends who also need to know Christ. Many times when a married person trusts Christ, their spouse and children will soon follow if we pray for them and talk to them.

Then pray for God to give you another soul this year. Just because you prayed for one, it doesn't mean you have to stop at one. God is glorified when you bear much fruit. (John 15:8).

7: Evangelism by Multiplication in a Nutshell

As a church leader who is starting Evangelism by Multiplication, you will focus on developing a core group of members who will make the commitment to believe God to help them bring one person to Christ this year - and every year - through their prayers and personal evangelism ministry.

You will challenge them, train them, pray for them and support them in their ministries. You will provide encouragement and reminders every week.

You will train them to walk in the Spirit and live a "Fruit of the Spirit" life that can compel some people to want to know more about knowing Christ.

You will train them:

1. How to pray for the lost
2. How to give their testimony convincingly
3. How to demonstrate the love of God in practical ways
4. How to live a compelling Christian life in the world
5. How to witness in the workplace
6. How to be friendly and start conversations with strangers
7. How to effectively ask evangelistic questions. Realize that the person who asks the questions is the person who controls the conversation.

8. How to start an evangelistic conversation
9. How to effectively and logically explain the Gospel
10. How to "close" the Gospel presentation
11. How to answer the questions unbelievers ask
12. How to defend the faith
13. How to disciple a new believer

In doing Evangelism by Multiplication, you will work to develop a culture in your church that is positive, uplifting, loving, extremely friendly, anticipating the moving of God, believing God and full of evangelistic fervor.

Evangelism by Multiplication is not another church program. It is an effective way to address the Divine Priority. We must treat the Great Commission that way.

As you develop the Great Commission-consciousness of your congregation, probably only about 10-20% of your people will buy in and commit at first. Most of those will be the people with the gift of evangelism. You will be giving them their track to run on. As they pick up the ball and run with it, you will see new people coming to Christ regularly. Little by little, other people in your church will catch the vision and commit to believe God for one soul to come to Christ every year.

We have learned by experience that people will respond more when we lead them with the simple baby steps of the Five and One Plan.

The goal is to see people coming to Christ every week, and getting assimilated into the church where they can grow in their faith. It is a very exciting experience for your church to watch new people being baptized every Sunday.

When I was a pastor, we kept the baptistery full all the time. We bought a swimming pool filter and chemicals to keep the water clean. During the best times of my ministry, baptism was a regular part of the service every Sunday morning.

Evangelism by Multiplication Is a Daily Lifelong Commitment

The Great Commission is not something to do once a year or every once in a while. It is our job always. Regardless of the kind of church program you have, your church has the responsibility to perpetually evangelize and make disciples.

In 1916, Henry Ford built a new factory for producing cars in Highland Park, Michigan. He had one goal for that factory - to produce cars. Lots of cars. He developed the first modern assembly line to produce as many cars as efficiently as possible. How often did they make cars in that factory? Every day. All the time. That is why Ford was so successful. Our job is to produce disciples and help them grow to maturity in the Christian life. Every day. All the time.

How Big Is Your Faith?

William Carey, who is known as the "Father of Modern Missions," was a man of great faith and great commitment to the Great Commission. One of his famous quotations is:

Expect great things from God.
Attempt great things for God.

William Carey expected great things from God, and he attempted great things for God himself.

He helped found one of the first missionary agencies. He went to India as a missionary himself. During his lifetime, the work he founded in India translated the Bible in 34 Asian languages, started many churches, and founded 19 mission stations, 100 rural schools and a weekly publication that is still published today. In the 1990's he was honored by the Government of India with a postage stamp that bore his image. He truly expected great things from God and attempted great things for God.

People are talking about the Western World being in the "Post Christian Era." The number of Christians in Europe and North America is dwindling. The things we have been doing to reach the unsaved with the Gospel in the past are not working. We have to explore new methods to get them to consider Christ. Worse yet, the things most churches are doing to keep their younger generations and reach them for Christ are a dismal failure. They don't have to be, but we need to wake up to reality. If we want things to change in the church, we have to change the way we see church, and we have to change the way we do church.

So then, what is your vision for your church? Is it merely to keep the program going and to keep the doors open? You might have to start there, but you don't have to end there. We serve a big God. He wants to do big things through your church. He wants us to believe Him for God-sized results in our ministries. Yes, God is interested in results. He wants us to bear fruit in our ministries.

God is in the business of changing people's lives with the Gospel. It is absolutely wonderful when one person finds life in Christ. It is 100 times better when 100 people find life.

God is looking for preachers and church leaders who will believe Him to do big things in their churches.

Believe God for God-sized results. Always believe God for results. Never stop believing God for results. Then go get 'em!

Section 2

Lighting the Fire

8: Start With Commitment and Prayer

Regular Prayer for People to Be Saved

"It is possible to move men,
through God, by prayer alone."
-Hudson Taylor, 19th Century Missionary to China

Hudson Taylor, the pioneer missionary to China and founder of the China Inland Mission, was used of God in the salvation of thousands of people in China during the 19th Century. In his personal experience, he saw many antagonistic people come to know Jesus through prayer.

There is a great sea of lost humanity within easy reach of most churches in the world. The first priority of your church is to reach those people, and to reach out from there. (Acts 1:8). Pray regularly for them to be saved.

Use the Five and One Plan. Keep a list of 5 non-Christians in your sphere of influence and daily pray for them to come to faith in Christ. As you pray for God to move on their hearts, watch for indicators that God is moving in their lives. It might not happen immediately, but it will happen. Some people will respond positively; some people will harden their hearts. Sometimes it takes years for them to respond. Some people will never repent, but our job isn't to save them, it is to give them the message.

How to Pray for the Lost

1. Pray that God will soften their hearts.
2. Pray that God will make them curious about the Gospel.
3. Pray that the Holy Spirit will convict them of their sin and their need for salvation.
4. Pray that God will draw them to Christ.
5. Pray that they will become more and more dissatisfied with their life as it is.
6. Pray that God will give you boldness and wisdom to talk to them about Christ.
7. Pray that God will open the eyes of their understanding of the Gospel.
8. Pray that God will help you find a natural opening to talk to them.
9. Pray the Isaiah 6:8 Prayer and surrender to God to go tell them.

> Also I heard the voice of the Lord, saying: "Whom shall I send, And who will go for Us?" Then I said, "Here *am* I! Send me." (Isaiah 6:8)

Prayer for Laborers

> Then He said to them, "The harvest truly is great, but the laborers are few; therefore pray the Lord of the harvest to send out laborers into His harvest.
>
> (Luke 10:2)

It is nice to have more musicians in the church; it is essential to have more soul winners. While it is good and important to pray for more teachers in the church when they are needed, that's not what this verse is about. Jesus was looking toward the vast fields of people who do not know Him. It was too big a task for His group of disciples to reach. It is too big a task for your church to reach. He is instructing us to pray for more laborers to work the fields - to reach the lost - for Him.

As you pray for more soul-winners in your church, where will you find them?

You start by training the people you have now. As your evangelism ministry bears fruit, train the new believers during their initial enthusiasm as Christians. God may also send some mature believers who are looking for a church that is serious about evangelism.

While it is not our purpose to take members from other Bible-believing churches, there are evangelism-minded people who are frustrated because there is no outlet to use their gifts in the churches they are attending. Some will be overjoyed to find a church where their evangelism gift is welcomed, appreciated and used.

Pray for your staff and members to win souls

All of your church staff members should be actively involved in evangelism and believing God for at least one soul per year. They are your church leaders. They should be leading the way you want your church to go - especially if your church is paying them a full-time salary. Give them time during their work week to evangelize. Pray together with them in every staff meeting, and pray for the people they are witnessing to.

Pray for power and boldness

> And when they had prayed, the place where they were assembled together was shaken; and they were all filled with the Holy Spirit, and they spoke the word of God with boldness.
> (Acts 4:31)

Most Christians are timid when it comes to sharing Christ. The Holy Spirit can give you boldness, as He did with the believers in Acts 4.

Teach your church to pray for boldness every day. Public prayers from the pulpit should also include the prayer for boldness. When God's people are filled with the Holy Spirit, they are given the boldness to share the Gospel with the lost.

Pray for wisdom

> If any of you lacks wisdom, let him ask of God, who gives to all liberally and without reproach, and it will be given to him.
> (James 1:5)

Ask God to give you wisdom in approaching people and sharing the Good News. Different people have different needs on the surface. Their central need, of course, is Jesus. Pray for wisdom to find their surface needs that they will respond to.

A number of years ago, one of my members had an unsaved husband. He was a "weekend alcoholic." He would stay sober during the week so he could work. Then he spent the weekends drunk. He did not own a car, so he walked to work.

I visited him on numerous occasions and tried to befriend him. He was always very friendly and respectful, but he would never respond to the Gospel.

One day I bought a new car. That evening I visited him, and again he was spiritually unresponsive. I didn't tell him about my new car. That was not the purpose of my visit. While we were talking, however, the Lord put a thought into my mind.

I asked him, "Ted, how much do you spend on booze every month?"

He said, "About $30 a week."

"Come here to the window, Ted," I said as I got up out of my chair, "I want to show you something."

When he got to the window, I pulled back the curtain and pointed to my car on the street. "Ted, I just bought a brand new car today. There it is." Then I continued, "My car payments are less than your beer payments. Why don't you get saved and buy yourself a car with your booze money?"

You should have seen the look on his face. He didn't know what to say. He did not get saved that night, but on Sunday morning he came to church and responded to the invitation for salvation. God instantly delivered him from alcohol. A couple weeks later he bought a new car and dedicated it to the Lord.

He later told me, "You know, Pastor, when you asked me that question, I couldn't get it out of my mind all week. I kept thinking how foolish I was to waste my life on alcohol when I could have bought a new car."

Ted became a very faithful Christian, and he became one of the leaders in our church. He was involved in Bible study every week until the Lord called him home, 25 years later.

It was not my wisdom to ask Ted that question that night at his house. I had been praying for wisdom, and the Holy Spirit directed me with the right words to say to penetrate his resistance.

Ask God for wisdom, and He will give it to you.

Pray for new believers to grow in grace

> And this I pray, that your love may abound still more and more in knowledge and all discernment, that you may approve the things that are excellent, that you may be sincere and without offense till the day of Christ, being filled with the fruits of righteousness which are by Jesus Christ, to the glory and praise of God.
> (Philippians 1:9-11)

Pray for them. Let them know you are praying for them, and let them know what you are praying. Pray with them. Pray for them to be fruitful Christians.

Often new believers begin having doubts shortly after they receive Christ - especially if their friends ridicule them or criticize their decision. It's kind of a spiritual "buyer's remorse," but it's more than that. Satan does not want them to grow and follow Jesus.

Some time back I saw a news story about a man who had murdered his best friend and his girlfriend. His friend had "stolen" her, and he wanted to get even. He got so angry he killed them both. When we rescue people from the Satan's domain, he gets angry, and he will do all he can to keep the new believer from actively following Jesus. We need to come alongside new believers, encourage them, and pray with them and for them.

9: Starting the Drive

If we are going to experience multiplication evangelism, we need to have multiple participants in our church evangelism team.

It has been estimated that about 10% of God's people have the spiritual gift of evangelism. This does not mean that they are the only ones who are responsible to evangelize. All Christians bear that responsibility. As a general rule, those with an evangelistic gift will be the first ones to respond to the challenge, and they will generally win more people to the Lord than the others in your congregation. After all, they are the ones with the special gift.

In the first stages, you will be challenging the whole church. If 10% of your people respond to the challenge, you are doing fine. Encourage the other people, but don't badger them. Work with the people who respond, and pray that the fire will spread throughout the church. Depending on your church's tradition and spiritual condition, this could take some time.

What about the other 90%? Get them on board by encouraging them to pray for people to be saved through this ministry. Ask them to be especially welcoming to the new people who will be coming in to the church through this ministry. Let them know that it will be a trickle at first, so they don't get discouraged if they don't see much in the line of results for a while.

Appoint a Director of Evangelism if you don't have one, and start regular meetings for training, encouragement and prayer. Use a good training curriculum.

For training curriculum ideas see
www.ChangeTheWorldTeam.com/resources

Launch Sunday: Morning

Plan a Launch Sunday. Preach a sermon on the general theme of "Each One Reach One," or something to that effect. In the sermon emphasize these themes:

1. God expects you to do something to effectively reach people and bring them to Christ.
2. He does not expect a whole lot from most people, but He does expect something from everybody.
3. When everybody does a little bit consistently, a whole lot will be accomplished.
4. Explain how multiplication works In evangelism
5. We are laborers together with God.
6. The call to action
    a. Make a list of 5 lost people to pray for.
    b. Commit to pray for them every day.
    c. Believe God for one soul you can win this year (and every year). Pray every day for one.

If everybody does a little;
Nobody has to do a whole lot;
And it is amazing what God will do.

Launch Sunday: Evening

On Sunday night, have a special training meeting for the people who respond. Some churches call this the *Front Line Group*. Other churches call it the *World Changers*. If fewer than 10% will respond, don't be discouraged. The most important thing is to start. Remember Gideon and his army. A handful of prepared soldiers plus God is a majority.

At the Sunday night meeting, select a convenient time and day to continue meeting. The meetings will be to train, to pray, share witnessing challenges, and for accountability.

Record all the training meetings - on video if possible. This will make the training available for review, brush-up, and to get new team members up to speed.

If 10% respond on your Lanch Sunday, that means 90% will not respond. That's OK. There are other things they can do that will be more comfortable for them to get started. Get them involved where they are willing. Your job as a leader is to give them an easy, non-threatening pathway to spiritual growth and productivity in the outreach ministry of the church. You want them to buy in to the process, even if they are not on the front line. There are three additional categories of jobs in the strategy: Prayer Warriors, Greeters and Friendly Members (which will encompass all of your members, hopefully).

Things to Teach to Your Front Line Group

1. How to win a soul to Christ. Share the Evangelism by Multiplication App. Have them role play, sharing the Gospel with the app. Then ask some volunteers to role play before the whole group.
2. How to start a conversation with a stranger and turn it to the spiritual
3. How to answer the tough questions and objections These would be questions such as:
   (add others as needed)
   a. Is there a God?
   b. Doesn't science disprove the Bible?
   c. What about evolution?
   d. If God is all good and all powerful, why does He allow suffering?
   e. How can a loving God send people to Hell?
   f. Why do Christians hate gays? (We don't hate them, but that is the question some people are asking).
   g. Why are there so many hypocrites in the church?
   h. What about those who have never heard the Gospel?
   i. Why do you say Jesus is the only way to Heaven?
   j. The Trinity does not make any sense to me
   k. The Bible has gone through so many copies and translations; nobody knows what it really says.
   l. Why did the church supress the "lost books of the Bible?"
4. Understanding people of other religions and philosophies and how to reach them for Christ
   (Emphasize whatever religions are prevalent in your community)

a. Roman Catholics
b. Liberal Protestants
c. Mormons
d. New Age
e. Jews
f. Muslims
g. Buddhists
h. Hindus
i. Atheists/Agnostics
j. Nones[6]
k. Iglesia ni Cristo (Philippines)

[6] "Nones" are people who claim to have no religious affiliation. They may or not be atheists. The are the fastest-growing religious classification in the US today.

10 The Evangelism by Multiplication App

The Evangelism by Multiplication App will make it simple for any Christian to share their faith with others.

If you haven't downloaded it already, you can download it for free to your smart phone or tablet, or you can scan the appropriate QR Code[7] on this page to install it on your device. (If you don't know what these are, that's OK. Just access the Google Play Store or the Apple App Store on your device). Once you have the app installed on your phone, you do not need to be connected to the Internet to use it.

Tap on HELP for a tutorial video. The tutorial is on our web site, so you will need to be online to see it.

www.ChangeTheWorldTeam.com

To make it easy for your congregation, you could print the QR Codes in your church bulletin if some of your people

[7] The square codes above are QR Codes. A person can scan a QR Code with an app on their phone. The QR Code will send to the web page where they can download and install the app.

know what they are and how to use them. Ask the "techy" people in your congregation to help the non-"techies" download the app.

Android Phones and Tablets

Apple iPhones and Tablets

Search for the Evangelism by Multiplication App.

You will find it under the name, Evangelism by Multiplication in the Google Play Store or the Apple App Store. The app logo is a butterfly.

The Gospel presentation uses the Bridge Illustration that is familiar to many Christians. It uses the diagram and appropriate Scriptures to explain the Plan of Salvation to an unbeliever.

It's easy to swipe from one slide to the next in the presentation. Even a new believer can lead a person to Christ with the app.

The app uses the Law to help unbelievers see their sin and their need of the Savior. For people who have been to church or who have been raised in a Christian culture, this can be very effective for establishing their need for Christ. When you get to the Ten Commandments slide, just point out one or two of the commandments that you think they might have broken.

> Therefore by the deeds of the law no flesh will be justified in His sight, for by the law *is* the knowledge of sin.
> (Romans 3:20)

Automated Follow-Up

The Red Button

Use the Red Button to send more information to a person who does not receive Christ when you are witnessing to them. Just ask, "Would it be OK if I send you some more information about Jesus, God and the Bible? If they say "Yes," then tap the red button and hand them the phone so they can enter their home and contact information.

The red button will show up on the slide where you ask them to receive Christ. If they indicate they want to receive Christ, ignore the red button and go to the next slide where you will pray with them to receive Him.

The Green Button

At the end of the presentation, after you have prayed with the person and shared the information to help them get started in the Christian life, you will see a green button. This button is for those who receive Christ through your witness.

Tap on the green button, and it will open to a form where the person can input their name and contact information. When they do this, it will trigger a series of emails. They will receive a short email lesson every few days to help them get started in the Christian life.

The red and green buttons will only work if you are connected to the Internet. If you are not online when you share the Gospel, write their information down, and then enter it when you are online.

The Importance of Automated Follow Up

An automated follow-up system seems a bit impersonal. That is not ideal. However, most people don't get any follow-up at all, and this is far better than none at all. This system will also help you when you follow up with your new believer, because it will augment your follow-up lessons, and it will encourage the new believer to go to church with you.

Whenever you lead a person to Christ it is vital to follow up with them. It's not enough to win them to Christ. Our job is to make disciples, to train them to follow Jesus and become mature, reproducing Christians. That is our responsibility after we lead them to Christ. If they are not willing to follow through, it is likely that they never understood the Gospel and never repented.

Section 3

Feeding the Fire

11: A Culture of Caring About the Lost

"Could a mariner sit idle
if he heard the drowning cry?
Could a doctor sit in comfort
and just let his patients die?
Could a fireman sit idle,
let men burn and give no hand?
Can you sit at ease in Zion
with the world around you DAMNED?"
--Leonard Ravenhill

Most churches only dabble at evangelism, if they evangelize at all. A pastor recently told me, "We're a Bible teaching church. We don't evangelize." The church was very small, but it owned a building, and it was big enough to pay the pastor a salary, so he was comfortable. Sadly, more than 1 million people lived within an easy drive of that church, and the church did not care enough to try to reach them.

Evangelism is Not a Church Program

Many times churches or whole denominations will have a special program for a year. During that year program they will emphasize one facet of the Christian life. At the end of the year, it's over, because it's time for a new program.

We cannot treat evangelism like that! There are only two times that we can take a break from purposely reaching out to people with the Gospel: 1) when everybody in our city is saved and is serving God; 2) when we get to Heaven.

Programs come and programs go. You probably can't even name the program you were so excited about 10 years ago. Evangelism must always be an everyday major priority.

Keep Evangelism on the Front Burner

It is so much easier and more intriguing to think about ourselves, our preferences, our needs, than it is to think about the people around us who need Jesus. Christians fall into that trap. Entire churches slumber in it also.

> and He died for all, that those who live should live no longer for themselves, but for Him who died for them and rose again.
> (2 Corinthians 5:15)

There are churches where the color of the new carpet is more important than the souls in their community. They deliberate and bicker over the new carpet and coldly let their neighbors perish.

Heaven is real. Eternity is long. People need Christ. Do we care enough to try to reach them? May God deliver us from a selfish life of self-satisfaction when people are going to Hell.

How Much Do You Have to Hate a Person?

Penn Jillette is an atheist, of the magician duo, Penn & Teller. Some time ago he made this statement:

> "I've always said that I don't respect people who don't proselytize. I don't respect that at all. If you believe that there's a Heaven and a Hell, and people could be going to Hell or not getting eternal life, and you think that it's not really worth telling them this because it would make it socially awkward—and atheists who think people shouldn't proselytize and who say just leave me alone and keep your religion to yourself—how much do you have to hate somebody to *not* proselytize? How much do you have to hate somebody to believe everlasting life is possible and not tell them that?
>
> "I mean, if I believed, beyond the shadow of a doubt, that a truck was coming at you, and you didn't believe that truck was bearing down on you, there is a certain point where I tackle you. And this is *more* important than that."

If we really believe what we say we believe about Heaven, Hell and salvation, how can we be silent if we really love the Lord?

If a cat suddenly runs out in front of your car, would you swerve to try to avoid hitting it? How would you feel if you ran over the cat? Would it bother you? Would it bother you more than if your neighbor or co-worker were to die without Christ?

That is why we must keep evangelism and making disciples the number one priority in our churches.

12: Accountability and Teamwork

People don't do what you expect;
they do what you inspect.
Dr. Elmer Towns, Liberty University

In order to make the Evangelism by Multiplication strategy work in your church, it must be:

- **Intentional** - You evangelize on purpose, or it won't happen.
- **Consistent** - Evangelism needs to be an everyday priority (Acts 2:47; 5:42).
- **Accountable** - Accountability leads to intentional, consistent evangelism.

Too many churches use the *"Dabble Dabble Plan"* for evangelism. They dabble a little here and dabble a little there. This inconsistency shows they don't think evangelism is important, and they are not serious about obeying God and rescuing people from Hell.

It is important to have a system of accountability. It shows that you are serious about multiplying your church's ministry, and it shows that you expect every member to be involved.

Evangelism needs to be a daily activity. Accountability needs to be weekly. We accept without question that worship services and offerings are normal weekly activities of the church. We must also commit to making evangelism and accountability standard weekly activities in our church. Ask everyone to participate. If anyone objects to the accountability, you can tell them you wish they would participate, but nobody is going to force them.

You are going to ask everyone to fill out a short form to report their evangelistic activity for the week. By doing this, you are letting your people know that you are expecting them to be involved in evangelism continually.

Pastors, staff members and board members have more responsibility as the leadership of the church. They should be required to put their names on the weekly forms. For other church members, it is voluntary.

Assign a team of people or the church secretary to total the results of the forms every week and record them. Do not get behind in the recording of the results, or it will communicate that your commitment to evangelism is sloppy at best.

Too often churches expect their people to witness for Christ, but they don't provide a framework to make it happen. It's not enough to tell our people. We must train them, encourage them, guide them, pray for them, pray with them and track their progress. Why do we need to track their progress? Because most people will make little or no progress unless they're tracked.

You can make it a competition to make it interesting. We are not competing against one another, but against ourselves as a church. We are keeping score as to how well we have done together. The more positive contacts we make for Christ, the more people hear the Gospel. As more people hear the Gospel presented in a clear compelling manner, more people will come to Christ. That is how we will fulfill our mission.

1. Every member hands in an evangelism activity form every Sunday.
    a. Name
        i. Pastor, paid staff members, deacons must give their name
        ii. For other members it is optional
    b. How many people witnessed to (attempted to share the Gospel whether you were able to give a presentation or not. This would include the presentations). Each attempt is called a *Start*.
    c. How many Gospel presentations where you shared the plan of salvation
    d. How many people invited to church
    e. How many tracts distributed
    f. How many people prayed to receive Christ
2. Keep track on a wall chart (Scoreboard) in the church with the total figures for the quarter, by the week.
3. Beneath the scoreboard
    a. Have a supply of report slips for people to fill out
    b. Have a box where people can drop their report slips through a slot in the top for privacy.
4. Pastor, at least once a month, from the pulpit, relate a witnessing experience you had during that month. Your people need to see you leading the way.
5. Set goals
    a. One tract distributed to a lost person per adult attender

b. One witness attempt per attender
c. One presentation per five or ten attenders
d. One invitation per five or ten attenders
e. Example – if your church has 100 adults in attendance
    i. 100 tracts given out per week
    ii. 100 starts (witnessing attempts) per week
    iii. 10 to 20 Gospel presentations per week
    iv. 10 to 20 people invited to church per week
f. Celebrate your church's success in meeting the goals

6. Be realistic
    a. You can't control the numbers of people who get saved. That is the accomplishment of the Holy Spirit working on people's hearts through your witness. We are laborers together with God. He is the One who gives the fruit.
    b. As a general rule, the numbers of salvations will increase with the number of Gospel presentations. The reason many churches don't see a lot of people saved is because they don't have a lot of evangelistic activity.
    c. As a general rule, the numbers of salvations will be lower at first due to several factors
        i. Many of your people are new and inexperienced at soul winning
        ii. Most people don't get saved on their first presentation of the Gospel. The seed has to be watered for a while before they are ready to respond to the Gospel.

iii. As your people get into the habit of witnessing, they will become bolder, more committed and more effective.

7. Objections - some people won't like this
   a. If they object, love them and tell them they are free to not participate if they are really against it. Tell them that if they can be more fruitful in effective evangelism by doing it another way, they have your blessing, and you hope that they will be actively bringing people to Christ. Do not be sarcastic when you say this. Be genuine and positive. We don't all have to do it the same way, but we all are expected to do it and bear fruit.
   b. If they are intent on opposing the ministry of Evangelism by Multiplication, be prepared for some of them to leave your church. Remember Gideon's army. You don't want them to leave, but it is important to build a team to do the work of the Great Commission in your church, and that it is better when there are no critical detractors to oppose the work of God. God has to come first. You'll never satisfy everybody. Jesus didn't either (John 6:66).

Weekly Ministry Report

Your name*________________________________

a. Witness attempts ...._____
b. Gospel presentations......._____
c. Invitations to church ...._____
d. Tracts distributed............._____
e. Prayed to receive Christ ._____

*Pastor, deacons and paid staff
.

Church Scoreboard

Date	Adult Attendance	Participants		Witness Attempts	Presentations	Invitations	Tracts	Salvation Decisions
1/3/16	100	54	54%	60	16	20	166	2
1/10/16	112	49	44%	38	14	18	212	0
1/17/16	106	56	53%	68	20	24	198	1
1/24/16	98	59	60%	73	22	26	184	2
1/31/16								
2/7/16								
2/14/16								
2/21/16								
2/28/16								
3/6/16								
3/13/16								
3/20/16								
3/27/16								

You can download the forms at:

www.changetheworldteam.com/tools-training/forms/

13: Keeping the Fire Burning

When a church starts to die, the first thing that drops off is evangelism. It's easier to care about ourselves and our needs than it is to care about our neighbors and their eternal destiny.

Therefore it is imperative to keep constant reminders before your people. They need to know that your church is committed to reaching people every week.

There are many ways you can keep it in front of the people every week. Here are some examples. You will doubtless think of many more as you implement them.

1. Banners on the church facilities.
2. Reminders in the bulletin.
3. Mention soul winning in every sermon, regardless of the subject or text.
4. Weekly training class for people to learn how to be more effective as witnesses
5. Mention evangelism in church newsletters, emails, blogs.
6. Recognize soul winners for their efforts from time to time in a service
7. Preach several sermons on evangelism and the Great Commission every year.
8. Print a quote about evangelism in every week's church bulletin
9. Baptize as often as possible. Highlight the soul winner who brought the new person to Christ.

10. Have the attitude that witnessing is as important to the Christian life as Bible study, prayer, church attendance and tithing. Speak about it in those terms.
11. Use music that reminds us of our responsibility to reach people for Christ.

Music

Music is a part of our worship to the Lord. We do that in church every Sunday. This is another purpose of music, however, and we need to use it for that purpose also in the church.

> Let the word of Christ dwell in you richly in all wisdom, teaching and admonishing one another in psalms and hymns and spiritual songs, singing with grace in your hearts to the Lord.
> (Colossians 3:16)

In addition to worship music that is addressed to God, we are to use music to teach and admonish one another in church.

During most of the 20th Century churches used many songs that admonished Christians of their duty to evangelize.. Many of the songs had to do with missions and our responsibility to evangelize overseas. Many others expressed our responsibility to evangelize at home. Most churches rarely sing those types of songs in their congregations today. Maybe that is because it is easier to worship than it is to win souls.

Some of the songs about evangelism and missions evangelism that were widely used are:

- Rescue the Perishing
- Throw Out the Lifeline
- Let the Lower Lights Be Burning
- Brethren, We Have Met to Worship
- Give Me a Passion for Souls, Dear Lord
- From Greenland's Icy Mountains
- O Christian, Haste, Your Mission High Fulfilling
- Must I Go, and Empty Handed?
- So Send I You
- We've a Story to Tell to the Nations
- Jesus Saves
- Far, Far Away, in Death and Darkness Dwelling
- Tell it Again
- Lord of Harvest, Send Forth Reapers
- Bringing in the Sheaves
- Whosoever Will
- Ring the Bells of Heaven

These songs kept the task of evangelism on the minds of Christians in church. We were reminding ourselves that we must reach lost people for Christ before it is too late. Many churches have lost that element in the contemporary Christian music they use, and they have lost their commitment to share the Gospel with the lost.

That does not mean we have to go back to the old songs, but it certainly won't hurt to sing some of them from time to time. It means we need to constantly include music with that message in our services, in the spirit of Colossians

3:16. Music is one more facet that God can use to keep our responsibility for evangelism on the front burner in our churches.

It is a good practice to use one song in every service that reminds us of our responsibility to evangelize.

If you do not keep evangelism on the front burner of your church, it will not be on the front burner in the minds of your people, and it won't happen in your church.

If you do not do evangelism on purpose,
You will not do evangelism at all.

14: A Visitor-Friendly Worship Experience

I may forget what you say
I may forget what you do
But I will never forget how you make me feel.
--Maya Angelou

People are emotional creatures. Most of the time we act based on our feelings. Advertisers and salespeople know that. If they can get you to feel good about them and their product, they are more than half way to getting the sale. Visitors to your church will form their opinions of your church and your message largely because of what they feel during the visit - especially during the first few minutes.

This may sound unspiritual, but God made us this way. When a lost person is under the conviction of the Holy Spirit, he or she *feels* the conviction, making them aware of their need of Christ. It's the way God made us. It's part of the way He works in people's lives. And it's the way people respond.

When people come to your church, they need to feel genuinely loved, respected and appreciated for themselves. They need to feel like they are important to God and to the people they meet in your church. They are important. They need to know that they are genuinely important to you - not because they are potential new members, workers or tithers, but because they are important to God.

We do not want to manipulate people's feelings when they come to our church. However, we want to make them feel welcome from the moment they drive into the church parking lot or step in the front door until the time they leave after the service. We want them to feel that we love them, and that our love is genuine.

When unsaved people visit a church for the first time, they usually don't expect much. We want to overwhelm them with the love of God through us. We want them to feel more loved and appreciated in church than any place they have ever been. This cannot be a syrupy put-on façade of love. It has to be genuine concern for them as individuals. We want it to be an unforgettable experience. We want to do this because we want them to know our Savior.

Definition of LOVE:
The conscious commitment
To the well-being of another
Regardless of cost to self

When we treat people with love, we listen to them; we have genuine concern for their feelings, their needs and their desires. Faking it does not work. It has to be the genuine love of God flowing through our hearts and our churches.

Some of your visitors may not look respectable. They may be living a lifestyle you do not approve of in your church. Teach your people to love them and to be non-judgmental toward them. Jesus loves sinners. We should too.

Guest Parking Spaces

Many churches have special parking spaces for first time visitors. Many visitors don't see the parking spaces and park elsewhere. Make sure your VIP Guest Parking Spaces are close to the door, and are easy to find for first time visitors.

It is important for the parking spaces to be close to the door for two reasons. First, you want to make it convenient for them when they come. Second, you want to make it easy for a parking lot greeter to spot them and meet them before they get to the door of the church. The parking lot greeter's function is to make them feel good about coming, and to be their "tour guide" so they know where to go, and where their children can go.

When people visit for the first time, they don't know where to go, and they don't know what to do. If they have children with them, they don't know if there is a special service or class for the children.

Make it easy for your guests to find their special VIP parking spaces. The spaces should be well marked. Your church people should know that they are never to park in the VIP spaces, even if they are bringing a guest with them.

You can paint a green line on the pavement from every parking lot entrance to the visitor parking spaces, and then post a sign at the entrance. Make it as easy as possible for them to feel at home when they come.

Whether or not you use a green line, make your visitor parking very easy to find for newcomers.

The Process for First Time Guests

Whenever possible, follow this procedure. Most guests come because a church member invited them. Train your people to either bring their guests with them or to meet them in the parking lot (or at the front door if it is raining).

In the Parking Lot

If their friend does not meet them when they park their car, a parking lot greeter should walk out to meet them. If it is raining, the greeter could keep an umbrella handy for them. The greeter should learn their names and greet each person in the family. The greeter should walk them to the information table near the front entrance and introduce them to a table greeter.

The Information Table and Gift Bag

The table greeter will give them a gift bag from the church. It is important to give them their gift bag *before* the service whenever possible. You want them to be carrying the gift bag as early in their visit as possible so that your people can notice them and greet them. The bag should include a church brochure, a Gospel tract, and a coupon they can turn in after the service for a free Bible if they don't have one, a pen, a visitor's registration card, a couple candy bars, a coffee mug or other gift from the church. The pen and coffee mug should be imprinted with the church name, city and logo. If the pastor has written a book, a copy of the pastor's book would be a great addition to the gift bag. Tell them the pastor will be happy to autograph it for them after the service if they would like. That will give them an incentive to meet and talk with the pastor after the service.

We do not want the visitors to feel that they are standing out, so we need to give them a gift bag that will make them noticeable in the church. A cloth tote bag with the church's name and logo will work very well. The bag should be red or another bright color that is easy to spot. It should be around 12 or 15 inches square, so that a woman will not fold it up and put it in her purse. All the bags should be the same color, and they should be bright enough so your people can easily see them. This will make it easy to spot the visitors who are carrying a bag, and the visitors won't feel like they are standing out.

Many church members would like to greet the first-timers, but in a medium to large church, it can be difficult to know who is there for the first time. It is embarrassing to ask a person if this is their first visit and then find out that they are a member of the church. Make it easy for your members to know and greet the first time guests. The guests will feel good about your church, and will be more likely to come back. Guests who are not Christians will be more inclined to listen to the message when they are treated well.

Investing in Your Visitors

Don't dismiss the importance of giving gifts to your visitors. A $5 or $6 investment in your visitors can go a long way, and it will more than pay for itself. Remember, every member you have was a first-time visitor at one time.

If finances are tight, think of it as an investment in your

church. An appropriate gift bag will make visitors feel really good, and it will help build bridges with them. Even though you tell them you do not expect them to participate in the offering, most people will feel like they want to reciprocate, without feeling pressured to do so. It's just human nature. You will probably break even, or at least come close.

Unsaved guests will be especially impressed. Remember, you want to do everything you can for them to have a good feeling about your church, as long as you don't compromise on your message or purpose.

> . . . every man *is* a friend to one who gives gifts.
>
> (Proverbs 19:6)

They will also build bridges to Christians who visit your church because they are looking for a church home.

In addition, you are putting things in the gift bags that will give people the information you want them to have.

After the Service

The first 10 minutes after the service are crucial if you want to make a good impression on first-time visitors. Before church everybody is getting ready for the service to start. After the service, most people are a little more relaxed and they have more time to talk with one another. Do you want your visitors to be lost in the crowd? Your greeters need to be busy greeting people again as they leave. This is a good time for members to introduce themselves to visitors. They will be easy for your members to identify, because they will be carrying their red gift bags.

The pastor should be available to meet the guests after the service. Train your members not to take the pastor's time after the service when there are guests he should meet and talk to. This is prime time for the pastor to connect with guests and to get to know them.

We want our guests to leave on a happy note. Make sure there are greeters at the door to greet them on the way out.

In addition to the parking lot greeters and information table greeters, you need greeters at all the entrances of the church both before and after the services. It is also good to have roving greeters. These should be the friendliest people in the church. They should not wear a badge showing that they are official greeters. They should just move through the people and spread good cheer. Their job is give a warm welcome to everybody they talk to. They should give special attention to the guests with red bags.

In one of the churches I pastored, we had an elderly lady who was super-friendly. She made everybody feel loved and important with a good word and a warm hug. Her joy was contagious. First-time visitors always mentioned her when we visited them later. We did not assign her that job, she took it upon herself. She was that kind of person. As a young pastor, I learned a lot from watching her interact with the people. We affectionately called her "the Church Grandmother." She loved it. Do you have any members like that? Set them loose! Give them the job of Roving Greeter.

If the guest has children with them, the table greeter will tell them what is available for the children and will get a volunteer to walk them to the nursery or the appropriate room(s) for the children's program(s). In addition, the greeter should point out to visitors where the washrooms and the sanctuary entrances are, if their locations are not obvious. Volunteers should be hanging around the table before the service starts for that purpose. Ushers should be on the alert for visitors carrying bags and should go out of their way to find seating for them.

You must train your greeters so they can have a positive effect on your church visitors. A greeter with an unkempt appearance, bad breath, too much cologne or a bad manner can turn visitors off.

You will see some resources for more information at

www.ChangeTheWorldTeam.com/resources

15: Evangelistic Appeal in Every Service

Regardless of the sermon subject, always incorporate an appeal for people to come to Christ. Make it urgent, because eternity is at stake for everyoneThere are a few reasons for this:

1. Your visitors may not be Christians yet.
2. It is possible that one of your church people is not a Christian.
3. It keeps your church focused on evangelism
4. It encourages your members to bring friends to church with them.

C. Sumner Wemp, one of my mentors, used to say, "It's a short trip to the Cross from any verse in the Bible." Whether you are preaching on tithing, on the family or on John 3:16, you can always close with an appeal to the lost to get saved.

The evangelistic appeal could be a traditional invitation to come forward and receive Christ. It could be an appeal to meet with a trained worker at a designated spot in the auditorium after the service. It could be a directive to meet a trained worker in a prayer room adjacent to the auditorium. Do whatever will be the most effective in your church. Just do something that works to bring lost people to Christ..

A worship service
Without an evangelistic appeal
Leaves God's business
Unfinished.

16: Regular Evangelistic Events

Quarterly Evangelistic Service

One Sunday morning each quarter, turn your morning service into an evangelistic event. Have a special speaker, a special musician, do something special to get people interested.

Sometimes it is difficult to get friends to come to church. They are not interested. If you give them a special reason to come, sometimes they will be interested.

It would probably be a good idea to not publicize this service as an "evangelistic service." We don't want visitors to think we are inviting them to proselytize them. (Unsaved people do not know the difference between proselytizing and evangelism).

> Surely, in vain the net is spread in the sight of any bird; (Proverbs 1:17)

Reasons to have a quarterly evangelistic service:

1. It gives your members a special reason to invite their friends.
2. It gives their friends a special reason to be interested and come.

3. When they come, the entire service is devoted to piquing their interest and sharing the Gospel with them. Much of the music should be about salvation and the joys of the Christian life.
4. Your members have an entire quarter to pray for the service, to pray for their friends to come with them, and to pray for God to open their hearts.

When to Have Quarterly Evangelistic Services

Schedule your evangelistic services for the times of the year that are the natural times for people to think about coming to church. In North America, the most natural times would be:

1. Easter
2. Beginning of Summer
3. Beginning of the School Year
4. Christmas

These might not be exactly 13 weeks apart, but they are spread out enough to work well. Easter is the easiest Sunday to invite people to church. Many people never think about going to church, except on Easter Sunday. Take advantage of that. Make Easter evangelistic. Have extra nursery and children's workers available. Pray and plan for a service that will make a big impact on many people's lives for Jesus.

If you promote it as a special service, make sure it is really special. Things you can do to make it special:

1. Famous Christian to give testimony
2. Christian local dignitary to give testimony

3. Interesting special speaker
4. Special soloist or music group
5. Christian with an interesting background to speak

If you don't have the budget yet to get a well-known speaker or musician, have the best musicians in your church put together a special musical program. Or, you could invite a person or musical group from a sister church with an interesting background to speak or give their testimony.

Promote the service like crazy.

1. If you have a special outside speaker or music, send a press release to all local newspapers and radio stations 2-3 weeks before the service. Most newspapers do not think of a church service as a newsworthy event, but a special speaker or musician is - especially if they are well-known.
2. Print up flyers or invitations for your members to hand out. Make sure the design and printing are good quality, as the quality of your printed pieces is a reflection on your church.
3. If you are a member of the Chamber of Commerce, take some invitations to the Chamber office 2-3 weeks before the event.

When I was pastor in London, Ontario, we had Dr. Clifford Wilson speak in our church. Dr. Wilson was the head of the Australian Archaeological Institute, and he was the author of several books refuting attacks on Christianity and the Bible. This was during the time that the book *Chariots of the*

Gods?[8], an attack on the Bible, was popular. Dr. Wilson had written a refutation entitled, *Crash Go the Chariots*[9], and he had overwhelmingly won a debate with the author of the other book. Dr. Wilsons's evidence was so overwhelming that Erich von Däniken, the other author, was afraid to debate him again.

I called one of our local radio stations and got him booked on a very popular talk show for one hour. I also got free TV time to conduct an interview with him on the local cable TV outlet. Clifford Wilson's appearance in our church was a newsworthy event, and we got a lot of free publicity. We had many visitors in church as a result.

Special Holiday Events

In addition to the quarterly evangelistic services, think about holidays that you can turn into evangelistic events. In the US, people celebrate Independence Day, the 4th of July. Our church has a large lot with a softball field. It is close to a fireworks display on the 4th of July. We have a picnic every year on the 4th, and then we watch the fireworks from our field. Your church can have a special event on a special holiday and invite your neighbors.

For Veteran's Day you could invite all the veterans in the community and have a special veteran speaker. Give each veteran special recognition and a small gift and/or a

---

[8] Van Däniken, Erich, *Chariots of the Gods?* 1968.

[9] Wilson, Clifford. *Crash Go the Chariots.* 1972.

certificate of thanks and recognition for their service to our country.

For the beginning of the school year, you can have an Education Day and invite all the teachers of all the schools in your community to honor them. Get the teachers in your church to help plan a meaningful experience for the teachers who will come. Special speaker for the day could be a teacher or retired teacher. Be sure to give them a small gift to take home with them.

I spent many years in Chinese churches in California. Chinese New Year is a natural time for a Chinese church to plan for an evangelistic event or pre-evangelistic event.

Movies

There are times you can rent a major movie that was shown in the theaters and show it in your church. Two of the recent movies that are available are *Son of God* and *God's Not Dead.* Schedule a time to show a movie in your church.

Print up free movie tickets and have your members distribute them everywhere. People love free movie tickets. Put an ad in your local paper. Serve popcorn at the movie for 25¢. Advertise "25¢ Popcorn" when you advertise the movie. People will talk about 25¢ popcorn more than they will about free popcorn.

When people come, tell them you will be doing more free movies from time to time, and that you want to make sure you can inform them of the free movies, so get their contact information.

Concerts and Other Performers

If you can get good Christian artists to do a concert in your church, get them. Make the events entertaining with a Gospel appeal. You are not limited to concerts. There are other types of Christian entertainers who can do a good evangelistic event for your church, including Gospel illusionists (magicians), comedians, etc.

Always have something going on to reach out to the people in your community. Your goal is to make friends with the people so that you can introduce them to our great Friend.

Seminars

What types of things are people in your community struggling with? Offer a free seminar. Dave Ramsey's Financial Peace University is very good for this. Parenting seminars can be good. If a lot of people are out of work in your community, you could offer a special seminar for them to help them. You could also offer a support group, and even a job fair. Do things to meet the needs of the people in your community to build bridges and help them see what Jesus can do in their lives. We have to show them that we care about them and their needs.

ESL Classes

Do you have a lot of immigrants in your community? You could host a daily or weekly ESL class. This is an ongoing event. You can also start an adult Sunday School class where the teacher teaches the Bible in simple English.

Do you have illegal aliens in your community? God loves them as much as He loves us. They are in your community so you can share Jesus with them.

You might not like the fact that we have so many illegal alien immigrants living here. That does not matter. Jesus died for them, and He gave us the Great Commission to reach them. The Jews didn't like the Samaritans. Jesus went to the Samaritan woman (John 4). In Acts 1:8, Jesus told His followers to take the Gospel to Samaria too. It does not matter what you might think of the illegals. Jesus loves them, and He died for them too. What can your church do to reach them so they can go to Heaven too?

Food Distribution

Is there a food bank that distributes free food for the needy in your community? Perhaps you could set up to be a place where people can come on a certain day of the week or month to get free food. You can give a Scripture portion and a tract to each person who comes for the food. Ask for volunteers to come to meet the people, witness to them and invite them to church.

Other Needs of Your Community

Your opportunities for ministry are not limited to those listed here.. Their need is our opportunity to introduce them to Jesus.

Obviously there are so many needs that your church probably cannot tacke all of them. Ask God to direct you to the ones that you are best equipped to tackle now. As you grow, you will be able to do more.

17: Up-to-Date Web Presence

Can people find your church online? What do they see? Will it make them want to visit your church? In the US and many countries, your web site is the most important thing you can do to tell the world about your church and interest them in visiting a service

Web Site

Almost everybody in the West today will check a church out on the web before they come to visit. This is happening more and more in developing countries too. If you don't have a web site, or if your web site does not look good, or if it does not quickly give them the information they want, they will probably decide not to come. Your web site is that important.

When a new family moves to your community and they are looking for a church, they will check on the web. Will they see your church there? What will they see?

Web sites are like fashions. The styles change every few years. If your web site is more than two or three years old, it looks old. It tells people you are out of touch. Your site should look up to date.

Many churches will have a member create their site to save money. Don't do that unless your member is a professional web designer. The web is so important these days; you cannot afford to skimp there. If you hire a professional web designer, plan to spend $500 to $2,000 or more for the site. Then it will cost about $50 to $100 per year to host it. That is the rent you pay to have your site on the web.

The Home Page on your web site is all about visitors and events. Give your non-members the information they need about your church on the home page. They don't have the patience to go clicking all over your site.

Journalists talk about the "inverted pyramid" when they write newspaper articles. The very first paragraph of their article is written to give you the information you need to know about their subject. They know that many people never read past the first paragraph, so they tell the whole story in the opening sentences. The rest of the article gives more detail. Your web site is like that. When a non-member first sees your web site, they should get all the information they normally would want to know on the home page. They should see pictures and copy that will make them interested in visiting your church. They should see the address and hours of services. If you have a special event planned, there should be something about the event. If they want more detail, they can navigate to the other pages.

They will not dig deeper into your site if they don't like what they see on the home page. Once they decide to dig (click) deeper, they are normally looking for a short statement of faith and the classes and activities you have for various members of the family.

Keep your web site up to date always. On two occasions I visited a church at the wrong time because the service times on the web site were wrong.

Some churches still have last month's events listed on their calendar of events. Assign a staff member the task of updating the online church calendar every Monday morning. If your webmaster has embedded Google Calendar into your web site, it will update automatically whenever you update your Google Calendar. You do not have to log into the site. It updates automatically.

Google is not the only company that offers this service, but Google is free, and it works very well.

You can also post recent sermons in audio or video formats on your site.

Use real pictures of real people on your site. If you can, put a good video on your web site. It is good to have a 1-2 minute video where the pastor gives a short greeting and an invitation to visit.

Mobile Web Site

Make sure your web site looks good on mobile devices. Over half of all web searches now are done with mobile phones and tablets, and that number is growing. Old web sites look terrible on the tiny screens. Today's web sites will automatically display differently on mobile screens so they look good and function well. The web sites that do this are called *Responsive* web sites, because they respond to the type of device they are viewed on.

Google Places

Have you ever noticed what happens when you look for churches in your area on Google? Normally the top of the page will feature a local map with a number of churches pinpointed on the map. Next to the map you will see the listings for the churches on the map. Does your church show up there?

The churches that show up there are registered on a free service called Google Places. Make sure you do that. If you do not know how to do that, just do a search on Google: "How to get on Google Places." You can learn how to do anything on Google.

Whatever you do, make sure your church is registered on Google Places, or a lot of searchers will not find you easily. They will likely find and visit another church instead.

Social Media

Do you have a Facebook page? This is a free place where you can promote your church. Teenagers and young adults usually know a lot more about social media than the older generation. This would be a good project for a teenager in your church. Have a policy about the types of things that can be posted. If you give the job to a teenager, make sure there is adult supervision. You don't want them to put the wrong material about your church on the Internet for the world to see.

Facebook also offers the opportunity to create a private Members Only group for the church membership to use.

Some churches create a Facebook page because it is free, and then they never keep it up. An incomplete outdated Facebook page creates a bad impression in people's minds. Wait until you are ready to maintain your Facebook page with interesting, relevant posts before you start one.

The parameters for Internet services - especially social media - are constantly changing. By the time you read this book some of the rules will already have changed. Be aware of this and try to keep track of these changes.

YouTube and Vimeo

You can put videos of your sermons on YouTube and Vimeo for free. A good online video project would be a series of 2-5 minute videos answering the questions that most people ask about the Bible, Christianity and your church. If the videos are optimized correctly, they can make your church show up more often on Google.

Reviews

Yelp is a web site where people can go and publish reviews about the businesses they patronize, as well as churches they visit. Many people rely on the reviews they see on Yelp.

Your church needs to set up its own profile on www.Yelp.com. This might involve starting from scratch, or "claiming" a listing that Yelp has already put there. This will include entering phone numbers, hours of services, pictures, and a good description of the church.

Every week, ask three or four of your members to write a review about the church on Yelp. While they are there, ask them to write reviews on a couple businesses they patronize. That will give their review of your church credibility to Yelp.

When they look at the other reviews of your church on Yelp, they can also post comments on the other reviews.

Your church should also post a link on its website so that anybody can leave a review. That way Yelp will know that you are not just looking for glowing reviews from members. The link on your web site will also make it easier for your members to find the right place online to post their reviews of the church.

Google also has a place for reviews. Ask your people to post their reviews there too. Again, the reviews should be spread out over time - a few reviews every week.

Email

You need to have a segmented email list (or multiple lists) so you can easily stay in contact with people. A segmented email list is a list that uploaded into a specialized bulk email service, called an autoresponder. A good autoresponder will allow you to send a bulk email to your entire list, or to one or more segments of your list.

For example, if you are promoting a Ladies' Meeting, you don't need to send it to the men. You can specify that you want the email to only go out to women. You can send another email that only goes to junior highs, to seniors or to singles.

Your standard email system that comes with your internet service cannot handle this efficiently if you have more than 20 people in your congregation. Powerful automated systems are very reasonable, and are quite user-friendly.

There is more information about email autoresponder systems available at:

www.ChangeTheWorldTeam.com/resources

18: Community Involvement

How visible is your church in your community? Do you participate in community events?

By joining and participating in the events of the Chamber of Commerce, you can build bridges to community leaders and business leaders. I had many opportunities to share my faith by being active in my local chamber. When one of the prominent business leaders in town committed suicide, I was asked to conduct his funeral. That gave me the opportunity to share the Gospel with about 100 of the leaders in our city, including the mayor, city council members and several other key leaders..

Most chambers of commerce have a monthly breakfast or luncheon meeting and a monthly mixer around 5:30 PM on a weeknight. It is a good place to build bridges. Your church could be the only church represented there, so you would be the one they would call on when they have needs.

Pastor Glenn Layne, formerly of First Baptist Church in Temple City, California, held a special meeting on a weeknight where he invited the city council members and all the other community leaders in the city. His church leaders also came to the meeting. The purpose of the meeting was to listen. He asked them, "What can our church do to better meet the needs of our community?" The response was very good.

Does your community have an annual parade? A

church float could be a good project. You probably won't see anybody come to Christ as a result of the float in the parade, but it will be a valuable way to touch the people in the community in a positive way. We need to do things to get the people in our community to like us when we can, and this is one of the ways. The parade float would be a good project for your youth group.

Do everything you can to be visible in your community in a positive way. This builds bridges that can enable you to reach more people for Christ, even though it might not result in immediate evangelism.

Does your community have a food bank or homeless shelter? How can your church be involved? The people in your community need to know that your church cares about them.

Do you have people in your church who could run for city council or the school board? It is important to get Christians into those offices. One Christian I know who ran for city council ended up in the US Congress a few years later. We need more people who can make a difference in government.

19: Branding Your Church

What comes to people's minds when they think of your church? What do you want them to think? Do they think of your church at all? Branding your church has to do with purposely creating the reputation you want your church to have in your outreach area.

Some churches are known for being negative and against everything. Some churches are known as being aloof and unfriendly. Others are known as being shabby, because of the condition of their facilities. What do people think when they think about your church? Or has your church made such little impact on your community that they don't think about your church at all?

The church in North America and Europe as a whole is doing very poorly in this area. Many people think of us as outdated, irrelevant and unnecessary. Homosexual activists have been successful at using the news media to convince many people that we are hateful because we don't support same-sex marriage. Militant atheists work hard at convincing the public that we are following a myth. The proponents of abortion publicize the notion that we are anti-woman's rights, and therefore anti-women.

To prove their points, the enemies of Christ point to the worst examples of churches they can find. Unfortunately, there are plenty of them out there. These efforts cause many people to think those things about us.

In addition to that, there are millions of former churchgoers who are no longer part of a church. Many of them were hurt in a bad church, or they had a bad experience in a good church. Some were just plain rebellious against God.

These are some of the factors that give church a bad reputation in the minds of many in our post-Christian era in the West. These are the things we have to combat.

So, what are we to do? You can't change people's minds about the church as a whole, but you can work to build the reputation of YOUR church by the ways you interact with your community and your commitment to help other people.

What Reputation Do You Want?

Here are some things to consider:

1. A church with meaningful and enjoyable worship services.
2. A church that loves people genuinely.
3. A church where people live their faith without hypocrisy.
4. A church where God is changing people's lives.
5. A church where people find hope.
6. A church that demonstrates that faith in the Bible is logical and rational.
7. A church that does not apologize for its stand on the inerrancy of Scripture.
8. A church that is not afraid to tackle the difficult questions people have about God and the Bible.
9. A church that has positive, engaging programs for children and teenagers.

10. A church that makes the community a better place to live.
11. A church that understands millennials and younger generations and effectively engages with them.

The public attitude toward homosexuality has made a drastic left turn since President Obama took office in the US. Gay marriage was unthinkable before 2008. Just 7 years later, we Christians are branded as "haters" because we oppose it. How do we handle that as a church? If the people in our community think of us as "haters," they'll avoid our church. On the other hand, we cannot compromise our stand. The abortion industry and the pro-abortion groups have also targeted us, but they have not been as vicious in their verbiage as the homosexual activists and the news media they influence.

We have to deal with the negative stereotypes if we are going to have a meaningful audience in our rapidly-changing world. What can we do?

The first thing we need to do is repent for our failure to evangelize and to be salt and light in our society. If we had been serious about evangelizing our communities and building disciples over the past 25 years, there would be so many Christians in the US that abortion and homosexuality would not be a public issue. We have forfeited our influence because we have not taken our responsibility to evangelize seriously. We have been following Christ halfheartedly while the enemies of God have been rallying their forces and building their strength against us.

Then we need to be careful about the stands we take in public. If the loudest voices people hear from our churches are about the things we are against, rather than the things we are for, we will build a negative image in the minds of the people we are trying to reach.

What do people need to know about us? They need to know that your church is the place where people find hope and healing. It is the place where people can find the amazing grace of God that changes lives. That is what we should have been doing all along. When people find Christ, their lives are changed. When multitudes of people find Christ, their communities and their nations are changed. When multitudes of Christians do not reach multitudes of lost people for Christ, there is something dangerously wrong in the church.

When the forces of evil are so great around us, it is an uphill battle to turn our Western nations back to God. But it can be done. God has done it before, and He can do it again. He will only do it when His people get serious with Him about their spiritual responsibility in the world.

We need to be outspoken for the love of God that changes people's lives when they are saved. Our message is one of hope and love and salvation. People need to hear that and to see it lived out in the lives of our people that it drowns out all the negative messages of the enemies of God.

So, where do we stand on same-sex marriage? We are against it. Where do we stand on abortion? We are pro-life. As important as these issues are, they are secondary to winning souls the building disciples. Making disciples and reaching our community for Christ are more important than anything else we can do in this life. When we, as the Christians in our country bring enough people to Christ and disciple them well, those problems in our society will begin to diminish.

We need to focus on changed lives for Christ. That is what happens when we preach the Gospel in power and sincerity.

Make sure your church is a place where people can find hope for their lives, their families and their future. Make sure your community knows that.

When one person gets saved, it changes a life
When thousands get saved, it changes a city
When millions get saved, it changes a nation.
When nations are changed, it changes the world.

20: How We Can Help Your Church

Change the World Team exists to equip pastors, missionaries and churches to equip their members to make disciples who make disciples who make disciples.

We will help you cast a vision to your members and train them for effective evangelism and follow up.

We can bring special training to your church and help you train your people and help them set the Godly goal of bringing at least one person to Christ every year.

We can help you keep the momentum going through prayer, encouragement and accountability.

Contact us now for information.

www.ChangeTheWorldTeam.com

bob@ChangeTheWorldTeam.com

Your Turn

My prayer is that you will lead your church into Evangelism by Multiplication so that it could be said of your church...

> And walking in the fear of the Lord and in the comfort of the Holy Spirit, they were multiplied.
> (Acts 9:31)

Let's change the world together!

Made in the USA
Monee, IL
08 December 2020